STEADY TILL
Sunset

OTHER BOOKS

By CHERYL JOHNSON BARTON

International Testimonies Series
His Praise Glorious
Yet I Will Rejoice
River of Delights
In a Besieged City

Missions History
Into All the World
With Lester A. Crose and Donald D. Johnson

Kid's Club Curriculum
Godcalling@yourheart.com 1
Godcalling@yourheart.com 2

STEADY TILL *Sunset*

By CHERYL JOHNSON BARTON

Warner Press
Anderson, Indiana

Coordinator of Publishing & Creative Services
Church of God Ministries, Inc.
PO Box 2420
Anderson, IN 46018-2420
800-848-2464
www.chog.org

To purchase additional copies of this book, to inquire about distribution, and for all other sales-related matters, please contact:

 Warner Press, Inc.
PO Box 2499
Anderson, IN 46018-2499
800-741-7721
www.warnerpress.org

Cover and text design by Carolyn Frost.
Edited by Stephen R. Lewis.
Interior photos by Cheryl Johnson Barton.

ISBN-13: 978-1-59317-546-7

Printed in the United States of America.

POD—LSI

DEDICATION

To God be the glory today, tomorrow, and
forever. For the journey—and the sure victory—
are not mine but his. Praise the Lord.

TABLE OF CONTENTS

FOREWORD

Foreword

To be able to paint word pictures of places, feelings, and experiences in such a way that the reader is both inspired and challenged is a gift. Blessed are the persons who can do so.

Cheryl Johnson Barton, my long-time friend and fellow missionary, is a person who does just that in this book of personal stories about her journey. With candor, she reveals her weaknesses, struggles, and insights gained. Most of all, she reveals her heart for God and her deep desire for ever-increasing intimacy with her Lord.

Cheryl makes no pretense of having "arrived," but she allows us to journey with her as she discovers God in the ups and downs of life. Although we have been friends for more than thirty years, I'm delighted to find that Cheryl brings fresh spiritual insight to each new conversation. May you share her joy of discovery as you read *Steady Till Sunset*.

Ann E. Smith*
Anderson, Indiana

---

* Retired Church of God missionary (Japan, 1951–77; South Korea, 1978–80) who has served as Cheryl's missionary mentor.

GROANINGS

The Spirit
Has promised
To intercede
With sighs
Too deep
Too deep
For words
Our words are
Too shallow
Our pauses
Too brief
Our hearts
Too broken
Our power
Too weak
Intercede
Intercede
We pray…
Intercede
Intercede
We pray….
Amen.

By Christie Smith Stephens*
Anderson, Indiana

---

* Christie, my fellow pilgrim on the journey till sunset, thank you for permission to share your heart's groanings (based on Romans 8:26–27) as an encouragement to all.

INTRODUCTION
Introduction

Completing this devotional book has taken several years of on-again, off-again writing. For one thing, it has never been an assigned project, something I could justify bumping ahead of many other tasks demanding my attention. Yet writing a sequel (of sorts) to my first devotional book, *Through a Glass Dimly* (first published in Japanese in 2003), was just something I wanted to do—for me—and maybe a few others would enjoy reading it too.

So, little by little, *Steady Till Sunset* began taking form through blogs, family letters, and personal reflections I jotted down on scraps of paper dug out of the recesses of my trusty, red backpack, which was eventually replaced, when my stiff shoulders and dignity caught up with me, with a much more age-appropriate purse. Even I had to admit that time was passing along and that I was no longer the twenty-something young woman who'd arrived in Japan in 1976 to begin a missionary career in a mysterious and unknown land.

As my husband Bernie and I passed the thirty-year mark of missionary life in Japan, we began turning our thoughts and dreams toward the United States as naturally as if we were homing pigeons at the end of our assignment. Having never pastored a congregation in the United States, we began to wonder about how that would be: a whole new adventure in ministry in our homeland, in a location and with a people we scarcely knew. Certainly we could speak much about Japanese and some other Asian cultures, but after spending our whole adult lives outside the United States, we wondered whether we had something—anything—to offer the church in America. After all, we were now receiving invitations to join AARP, eat off the senior menu (which just seemed to be a summons to pay more money for less food), and listen in on discussions about whether there is any place for seniors in America's job force today—not the most uplifting of discussions for someone in her mid-50s and approaching a career change at such a late stage in life. Nevertheless, excitement was in the air.

And then came cancer—renal cell carcinoma in my left kidney, diagnosed in March 2009. Suddenly, everything was different. While I didn't have any miraculous revelations from heaven, one day I realized that I had to get my thoughts for this book organized and in a presentable form that might also speak to others on their own life journeys—whether confronting cancer or any other major challenge God allowed them to face.

What follows, then, in these thirty-one devotionals is a chronicle, not only of the cancer journey, but also of my personal journey as a missionary (1976–79; 1982–present) of the Church of God (Anderson, Indiana). To be sure, much more could be written in these pages. Even if you are not a cross-cultural missionary or have never been one, I believe these devotional articles will help you in your own walk with Christ, for they are reflections on many aspects of the Christian life.

I trust these also will be challenging to family, friends, and others I may never know personally. Jesus Christ lived thirty-three years on this earth to proclaim the message, "I am the way and the truth and the life. No one comes to the Father except through me" (John 14:6). May you, too, come to accept and walk hand-in-hand with my Lord and Savior, who loved me and drew me to himself so many years ago in order that I may remain "steady till sunset," whenever that sunset may be.

Cheryl Johnson Barton
December 18, 2010
Anderson, Indiana

$\mathcal{W}eek$
ONE

Themes: *Praise, Evangelism, Missions, Gratitude, The Tongue, Trust, and Complaining*

JARS OF CLAY

Jars of Clay

Theme: Praise

Bible Reading: Psalm 150; 2 Corinthians 4:7–9, 16–18

ut we have this treasure in jars of clay to show that this all-surpassing power is from God and not from us" (2 Corinthians 4:7).

It could have been yesterday. That's how clearly I remember it; that's how painfully I still feel it.

Bernie and I were new missionaries. We'd arrived in Japan six months after we were married, fresh from college graduation. We were nervous about our new assignment at Saga English Center, Saga University, and Saga Church of God, but we had the confidence of youth on our side. It was an assurance that said, "I can do anything," although we weren't brash enough to announce that out loud.

It didn't take long to get the wind knocked out of us. We were still adjusting to married life—and now in a new culture. We couldn't speak Japanese and had few English-speaking friends. We hadn't brought enough money to get us to our first paycheck, so we were eating only rice and vegetables. And then there was that October Sunday when only five people, including us, came to church. On our first Sunday, more than thirty people had gathered. Had we killed the church by coming to Japan?

Beyond this, there was difficulty with our boss. He wanted us to work on a Sunday. Granted, it was to judge a once-a-year speech contest, but our concern was the precedent it might set that the school could require us to miss church at any time. We were standing firm and certain we were right—until our missionary mentor advised us to judge the contest. It sounded like blasphemy to us. No one understood our position that we'd thought was unquestionable.

It's been a long time since I was a rookie. After more than thirty years in Japan, Bernie and I serve as mentors now. Thank God that we can relate to the younger missionaries because we remember well our own feelings and experiences.

But it's still not a carefree life, no matter how long I've been a missionary. I think of the kindergartener who did everything he could to disrupt a children's program I was involved in recently. My inability to control him—and, more importantly, to love him—devastated my confidence that I should ever try to teach children again. My legs were knocked out from under me. Good thing, too. It's much easier to begin praying on your knees when you're already on the floor.

Every missionary knows exactly what I'm talking about. So does every Christian. God has called us to do far more than is possible and with far fewer resources than we need. This is why we relate so easily to Paul's words, although sometimes we feel not just like jars of clay but like broken ones. Praise God that his power, abilities, and resources never fail, even when ours do. As Paul also said, "I delight in weaknesses, in insults, in hardships, in persecutions, in difficulties. For when I am weak, then I am strong" (2 Corinthians 12:10).

To Ponder: Have I ever felt like a broken jar of clay?

To Pray: Lord, to be honest I'd rather ask for strength than praise you for my weaknesses. Strength and self-sufficiency seem much more admirable than weakness. But I want to be your obedient and trusting child. This comes through praising you in every circumstance. May I be faithful. In Jesus' name, amen.

ON CASKETS AND CALLINGS

On Caskets and Callings

Theme: Evangelism, Missions

Bible Reading: Matthew 28:18–20; Luke 9:23–26

*C*askets. I've been told that missionaries of bygone eras packed for their assignments in caskets—their own. There was no sugar-coating the truth that answering the call to missions was a lifetime commitment. To fulfill this, these stalwart men and women were prepared to give their lives—literally. Not a few were buried on foreign soil, the news of their passing not reaching their faraway loved ones for months, perhaps even after grass had begun to cover their burial plots.

The Victor Maiden family is one example in the annals of Church of God missions history. Victor and Florence and their four children sailed from the United States for India, arriving at their final destination in the northeastern state of Meghalaya in 1906. But after only six months there, the two oldest children, a boy and a girl, died from malaria. Their funerals were hardly finished before a second son died three days later, and a short three weeks after this, Florence also succumbed to malaria.

Unbelievably, more grief and pain were ahead. Within another week, Victor buried his only remaining child, a five-year-old boy. Even then, although he changed locations and assignments, he didn't turn his back on what he believed was a nonnegotiable and forever call to India. Faithfulness to that call cost him his own life one year later. The entire Maiden family is buried in a cemetery in Meghalaya's capital city, Shillong, a bittersweet testimony of the price some have paid to proclaim the gospel in foreign lands.

Sometimes I feel really soft. Although we've spent many years in Japan, it's never really cost us much. We've missed some births and weddings we'd have liked to celebrate with family and friends and the funerals of five of our grandparents and a niece. But actually, living in one of the most modern nations of the world, we know little of true sacrifice.

I feel this all the more as I reflect on a quick trip to Guam to visit our son. Only a three-hour hop from Tokyo, the island is close enough for an occasional get-away from the grind of the big city. It's never difficult to trade crowded trains for nearly deserted beaches and Tokyo's gray skies and nondescript buildings for colorful fish playing hide and seek in the coral reef, velvety blue starfish hugging the sandy ocean floor, and the wide open canopy of clear blue skies. If I could, I'd jump on an airplane tomorrow and return. Or I'd fly three hours in another direction to see our daughter. While goodbyes are never easy, I'm happy I can say hello often. Still, I'm a little embarrassed and wonder if I'd have signed up to be a missionary in another generation.

Sometimes I remember that Jesus said, "If anyone would come after me, he must deny himself and take up his cross daily and follow me" (Luke 9:23). Having just returned from a beautiful tropical paradise, I'm pretty sure the cross he meant wasn't made from palm trees.

To Ponder: What cross must I bear today?

To Pray: Even if you're only calling me to visit a neighbor down the street, you are calling me, Lord. I confess my deafness to your call. Truthfully, I'm terrified of bearing a cross. It sounds so painful. But it's what you've asked me to do. Help me obey. In Jesus' name, amen.

TELLTALE SIGNS

Theme: Gratitude

Bible Reading: Psalm 100:1–5; 1 Thessalonians 5:16–18

The coughing started in September 2008. We'd just returned to the United States to visit supporting churches—something we do as missionaries every two years. I thought it was no big deal but went to the doctor as a precautionary measure in October. "It's probably allergies," he responded easily after examining me, noting that Indiana was experiencing an especially horrible allergy season. "It'll probably clear up when you leave Indiana."

Only it didn't. As we prepared to return to Japan in November, I saw the doctor again. Although still not concerned, he agreed to more aggressive treatment to ease my mind. He prescribed a heavy-duty cough syrup, gave me an inhaler, and ordered a lung X-ray. I was happy the X-ray was clear, but neither syrup nor inhaler alleviated the cough.

In fact, the coughing bouts increased. In December, they were joined by heaviness in my chest, even pain, when I exerted myself. Gradually, my energy flagged as well, until the January day when I began crying as I admitted to my father on the telephone, "I'm just so tired. I can't seem to do anything without resting. But I've got two book deadlines and I've got to keep going."

What would a girl do without her father—even a girl as old as I? I'd been married thirty-three years to a wonderful, loving, and caring husband, had been blessed with two children and a cute grandson. (Now I have two grandchildren.) But at that moment, it was Dad who brushed away my tears, prayed, and comforted me the way all loving daddies do when their little girls hurt. Never mind that he was half a world away in the United States.

But still the coughing didn't stop. Finally, with the books off to the publisher, I began a month of weekly hospital visits in February. Gradually, the respiratory doctor eliminated pneumonia, bronchitis, whopping cough, viruses, and asthma. Yet the cough was worse and blood work showed anemia and highly elevated CRP. Something was wrong, but there were only telltale signs. Two weeks before a sonogram of my kidneys finally led to diagnosis, Dr. Yamamoto said carefully, "Muzukashii byoki kamoshiremasen." Instinctively I knew he was suggesting the strong possibility of cancer.

One week after my hospitalization in April, I was home resting, less one kidney, and awaiting the pathology report from the surgery. Amazingly, my cough disappeared after surgery, I no longer panted when walking, and my energy was returning. Although I knew that untangling my thoughts and emotions was going to take time, I realized something already: I was overflowing with gratitude for telltale signs that led me to a good doctor and a good hospital. Most of all, I'd been overwhelmed by the love of friends and family from Japan and around the world, especially the family of God. I was speechless with wonder for I knew I'd done nothing to deserve all this. As my emotions swelled, I realized I'd seen the invisible God. His name is Love (1 John 4:8).

To Ponder: For what am I grateful?

To Pray: Loving Father, there is so much for which I am grateful: salvation through Jesus, enduring hope in you, my earthly family, my Christian family, and...(name these things now). Help me also to be grateful for my trials through which you come to me. In Jesus' name, amen.

JUICY GOSSIP

Theme: The Tongue

Bible Reading: Ephesians 4:29–32; James 3:1–12

elephone—the name of a game we sometimes played in youth group when I was a teenager. One person whispered a "message" into the ear of another, who then quietly passed on what he'd heard to the next person. Each subsequent player did the same until the message traveled around the room. Often, when the last teen announced what the first had said, the room erupted in laughter because the final message was so different from the first. Like juicy gossip, the truth had been distorted terribly.

On May 16, 2009, Bernie and I went to the United States for a second opinion about the kidney cancer treatment I'd had in Japan in April. There was the possibility I might remain for further treatment, but since the results of a PET scan in May showed no metastasis, the likelihood of that was slim.

Happily, the American doctor concurred with my then clean bill of health and agreed that, as long as the cancer didn't recur, I only needed regular checkups. Feeling like gold medalists in a marathon, Bernie and I flew back to Japan according to plan and made my first checkup appointment for the end of July. It was almost as if I'd never had cancer at all.

Imagine my surprise in June when I called a friend in Kyushu and discovered that the news she'd heard was completely different.

"It must be really difficult, isn't it?" she asked, her voice full of concern. I had no idea what she was talking about and told her so.

"What?" she replied, obviously startled by my puzzlement. "Where are you?"

"In Tokyo," I laughed, wondering where the conversation was going.

"I thought you were in America getting treatment," she explained. Now we were both completely confused.

Slowly I began to unravel the puzzle. An unexplained spot on my lung had concerned my Japanese doctor. But the American doctor identified it immediately as the aftermath of histoplasmosis, an environmental disease common in my birth state of Indiana and its neighboring state, Ohio. In most cases, including mine, the victim never knows she's contracted it since the body heals itself. The only evidence is the calcium left behind after healing. Although we'd shared the news happily with friends all around the world, somehow the story hadn't been able to travel the 565 miles between Tokyo and Saga without morphing into a new version: I was battling for my life in America and unsure if I could ever return to Japan. I could only shake my head in wonder.

In my case, what happened was completely harmless and amusing. But it's not always this simple. Careless words and juicy gossip often wreak havoc and cause pain for a lifetime. No wonder the Bible cautions, "Consider what a great forest is set on fire by a small spark. The tongue also is a fire...[and] no man can tame the tongue. It is a restless evil, full of deadly poison" (James 3:5, 6, 8).

To Ponder: Do I enjoy passing on juicy gossip?

To Pray: Stretched truths, gossip, white lies—they're all the same to you, Lord God. They're sin, and I'm guilty. Forgive me and purify me so that my mouth will always honor you and never shame you. I need your help, for I cannot change without it. In Jesus' name, amen.

LESSONS FROM THE MOUNTAIN

Lessons from the Mountain

Theme: Trust

Bible Reading: Joshua 1:1–9

*M*t. Fuji. Without doubt, this mountain is one of Japan's most magnificent and beloved national symbols. In September 2007, I spent five days on its patio. It was a wonderful personal writing retreat only a stone's throw away from the mountain's grandeur. Looking out the window, I felt the mountain's strength because of its close proximity—when I could see it.

Actually, Mt. Fuji danced with the clouds all week long except for Monday, when I arrived in Fujiyoshida by a quaint, two-car train and had my ticket punched by a real person instead of an automated ticket wicket—the way it always was when we first lived in Japan thirty years ago. Mostly the clouds won that week.

On my second morning, unable to see anything of the rocky mountain, I contemplated the lessons I could learn from the thick shroud that blocked even a glimpse of it. Here's what I wrote in my notebook: (1) Mt. Fuji is there, even though I don't see it; (2) It's close, even when there's no evidence that it exists; (3) The fog and clouds don't change the mountain at all; and (4) I will see the mountain again.

Thursday morning, after a typhoon passed, Mt. Fuji began peeking out occasionally from under the cloud bank as if gauging whether it was safe to emerge again. By the afternoon, the sky was a hazy blue, providing a gorgeous picture frame for the distinctively shaped mountain. That evening, as I walked at sunset, a rosy coloring set off the top of the mountain from the darkening sky.

While I could easily have spent my final evening reveling in Mt. Fuji's beauty and the hint of fall in the air, especially after a very productive week, I found my thoughts turning elsewhere: to my friend whose husband beat her, to another whose home life was threatening, and to a third acquaintance whose husband just had been convicted of a crime his family was sure he never committed. There was no rosy hue on top of a picturesque mountain in their homes that evening. As dark as things were, the only mountain they could see was one of defeat and discouragement. What could I say to encourage these three women? I was at a loss for words.

Suddenly I remembered the lessons from Mt. Fuji. Eagerly, I called out to my sisters from my heart. Remember! God is present, even though you don't see him now. God is close to you, even when you find no evidence at all that he exists. The dark valley in which you've been thrust unwillingly doesn't change God in the least. Finally, you will see God again. I promise you. Better yet, the Bible promises you.

Hold fast to these truths, beloved, even in the midst of your storms, and take comfort from *his* words to you, "Be strong and courageous. Do not be terrified; do not be discouraged, for the LORD your God will be with you wherever you go" (Joshua 1:9).

To Ponder: Of what am I most afraid?

To Pray: Joshua was terrified as he faced the enormous responsibility of leading the children of Israel. Just when he needed it most, you assured him that you would be with him. Lord God, help me to trust that your promises to Joshua are also for me. In Jesus' name, amen.

AT SHIBUYA CROSSING

Theme: Evangelism, Missions

Bible Reading: 1 Chronicles 16:23–29; Luke 13:34; 19:41

*O*vercrowded. Jam-packed. Teeming. Swarming. Busy. Congested. Crammed full. Packed out. Suffocating. All of these adjectives and others could describe Tokyo, the city in which we've lived since 2003. And did we say it's heaving with people here?

Whatever the verbal portrait, words just can't convey the experience of being in Japan's most populated city: 12.5 million at night and 14.6 million by day, when commuters from surrounding areas fill the trains beyond capacity to make their way dutifully into the city for work. Largest of the nation's forty-seven prefectures in population, Tokyo is its third smallest in geography, accounting for the dubious honor it holds as Japan's most densely populated location

(2,215 people per square mile). But as I said, words don't do it justice. You just have to experience it.

Which is what we did one Sunday afternoon when we went to Shibuya, one of the major downtown areas, only a ten-minute train ride from us. Shibuya Station itself was busy enough to make me wonder whether we should have taken out travelers insurance. But exiting the station and coming face-to-face with Shibuya Crossing was even riskier, just a few steps to be sure, but definitely not for the faint-hearted. Three million people—one-fourth of all of Tokyo—cross the street in all directions at this crisscross intersection made famous in the United States by Bill Murray's 2003 movie *Lost in Translation*. That's a swarm of 1,500 people traveling every time the light changes! And there we stood, trying to take a picture in the midst of it all.

Task finally accomplished, I stepped up out of the fray and positioned myself on the edge of a large concrete planter where I could get a good view and comprehend what I was seeing. It was then that I began to notice faces. Beforehand, there had only been a mass, a sea of humanity that didn't seem human at all. But from my elevated perch, I began to see—really see—for the first time: the pleasant man who looked up and smiled, prompting me to return his greeting and enjoy his jaunty gray felt hat with the feather stuck in its brim; an elderly couple, she bent by osteoporosis, he gallantly defending her as they navigated the treacherous crossing; the cute little boy with contemplative eyes being piggybacked in a child carrier; the teenager with her shaggy-cut, turquoise-dyed hair, a red and black plaid scarf wrapped around her neck; the surprising young man, his hair arranged in a mohawk of six-inch red, black, and gray spikes, his black jeans so weighted with chains I marveled that he could walk, much less keep his pants up.

I recalled Bernie's comment as we'd eaten lunch a few minutes earlier at Yoshinoya, a Japanese fast-food rice-bowl eatery, "How is it possible to reach some of these for Christ?" And I wondered: if Jesus had been standing there instead of me, would he have wept over Shibuya as he did over Jerusalem? Surely.

To Ponder: Have I ever wept because most of the world doesn't know God's saving love, mercy, and grace?

To Pray: Make me cry, Lord God. I know I should tell others about you, but this will never happen until I love and care for them as Jesus did. Break my heart for the world, I pray. Then help me to share your love with someone today. In Jesus' name, amen.

CONFESSIONS OF
A CRYBABY

Confessions of a Crybaby

Theme: Complaining

Bible Reading: Hebrews 12:1–3; Philippians 2:14–15

One of my favorite books that we read to our children when they were growing up is titled *Cloudy with a Chance of Meatballs*. All the weather in the fictional town of Chewandswallow was food. It came three times a day: at breakfast, lunch, and dinner. So no one ever had to cook, which sounded great to me. The weather rained soup and juice, snowed mashed potatoes and green peas, and occasionally there was wind that blew in storms of hamburgers, pancakes, or sausages. On one of the worst days, spaghetti tied up the town. We enjoyed laughing at the weather with Ben and Stephanie, our children.

But some days the weather isn't laughable. Rainy season in June is bad enough; it's worse if it keeps on going into July. Then comes the nearly unbearable heat and humidity of summer. But finally it's October, my favorite month of the year: clear blue skies and temperatures that are just right—cool in the mornings and evenings, and warm, but not too hot or humid, during the days. Only things went haywire in October 2007. I could have written a book called *Cloudy and Rainy with no Chance of Clearing.*

Which is why I happily discovered some notes I'd written earlier that year after walking in our neighborhood. I'd been struck by the abundance of colors I'd seen and had jotted these notes in my date book: a red mailbox; purple hydrangeas; a green signal at the corner; red geraniums in window boxes; fresh spring-green trees; the burnt red brick sidewalk leading to the brown boardwalk around the park; a clear stream reflecting the bright blue sky; an iridescent dragonfly flitting between lavender water irises; a father and son playing catch together, their orange and green baseball caps announcing their favorite baseball teams; pink roses; a triangular red stop sign; and purple, pink, and white pansies at our door.

I'd also scrawled six more words on the scrap of paper I'd found somewhere: the myth of the gray city. What in the world was I thinking? I wondered as I reread it in October. This gray city is no myth. Tokyo is a concrete jungle, and on rainy days the gray is grayer yet. (At such times, the laundry basket overflows and clothes hang all around the apartment to dry, even though that is practically impossible in such high humidity that gives me a headache and makes the air as heavy as my backpack full of groceries.)

Looking more carefully at what I'd written, I saw another notation: "Let us fix our eyes on Jesus, the author and perfecter of our faith…" (Hebrews 12:2).

Suddenly, I remembered the lesson I'd contemplated that beautiful spring day. It is not a question of gray versus the brilliant colors of the rainbow. Color is all around me, even in the gray city. The question is, where will I fix my attention? It's a choice I make every day, and it affects all of life, not just my thoughts about the weather.

To Ponder: How much is complaining a way of life for me?

To Pray: Forgive me, Lord, for my complaining attitude. Help me instead to focus my eyes on you and to choose praising instead of pouting. This not only will please you, but it also will lighten my heart. I start now with these words of praise: _____. In Jesus' name, amen.

Week TWO

Themes: *God's Love, Praise,*
The Church, Trust, and God's Mercy

THE FINGERPRINT

Theme: God's Love

Bible Reading: Isaiah 53:5–6; John 3:15–17

How such a simple process could have become so disorganized and complicated was beyond me. But my serving partner seemed completely unaware that trays of Communion juice and bread were stacking up against each other in the middle of the rows of benches as if they were vehicles being swallowed up in an unending traffic jam. No matter how I tried to catch his attention from the other end of the pew, he kept his eyes lowered reverently, seemingly oblivious to the growing problem.

It got so confused that one row of congregants didn't receive a plate of bread until everything was almost over. When I suddenly realized they'd been overlooked, I nearly sprinted from the back of the sanctuary to serve them before the prayers began. If the worshipful mood hadn't already been broken, I certainly succeeded in shattering it then. At least the quietness of a holy moment was destroyed for me.

Heart pounding and cheeks red with embarrassment as I sat down, I took the bread in my left hand and the tiny cup in my right, nestling it between my thumb and first finger. It was then that I saw the print of my pointer finger. Amazingly, the juice was reflecting it as my finger rested on the outside of the cup. It was as clear as if a detective had dusted the vessel for fingerprints and determined beyond any doubt that suspect Cheryl Barton had indeed held that glass cup that particular morning. I'd just been identified in the police lineup and there was absolutely no use in denying my crimes. My fingerprint was the proof required.

Amazingly, rather than the remorse and fear of punishment I should have felt then, I was flooded with the most beautiful feelings of love I've ever experienced. Jesus enveloped me in an amazing hug, his nail-scarred hands rubbing my back gently and lovingly. Rejoicing, I was reminded that it is for such intimate moments with God that we were created; it is for these pinnacle experiences that our hearts yearn.

And then I heard him as clearly as if he were sitting immediately beside me, whispering into the ear of my heart: "See your fingerprint?"

Of course. It stood out on the cup as if painted in the bold and decisive strokes of calligraphy, only in opaque ink rather than *sumi*, a traditional Japanese ink made from charcoal.

"This is my blood shed for you. It has your name on it, just as your fingerprint does. This is how much I love you."

And from deep within, my soul rejoiced as the words of a familiar hymn came into my mind:

When peace like a river attendeth my way, when sor-rows like sea billows roll, whatever my lot, thou has taught me to say, It is well, it is well with my soul. It is well, it is well, it is well, it is well with my soul.

Though Satan should buffet, though trials should come, let this blessed assurance control, that Christ hath regarded my helpless estate and hath shed his own blood for my soul. It is well, it is well, it is well, it is well with my soul.

My sin—O the bliss of this glorious thought!—my sin, not in part but the whole, is nailed to his cross and I bear it no more. Praise the Lord, praise the Lord, O my soul. It is well, it is well, it is well, it is well with my soul."*

Hallelujah and Amen!

To Ponder: When was the last time I felt enveloped in God's arms of love?

To Pray: Oh God, how I long for such intimate moments with you. Far too often I am satisfied with doing Christian things rather than with being with you and rejoicing in your limit-less love and forgiveness. Teach me, I pray, how live in love with you. In Jesus' name, amen.

---

* "It Is Well with My Soul." Lyrics by Horatio G. Spafford, 1873.

WHEN GOD SAYS NO

When God Says No

Theme: Praise

Bible Reading: 2 Samuel 12:13–20

*I*n November 2006, I visited India to encourage some missionaries in their work with Tibetan Buddhists. With only one thousand known Tibetan evangelical Christians in the world, my friends labor in a very difficult location despite personal danger, persecution, unresponsiveness, and austere living conditions. It had taken five long years to lead one Tibetan to Christ. Amazingly, he was a monk in the Dalai Lama's temple in Dharamsala.

Not long after he came to Christ, Pema* began experiencing a variety of physical and emotional illness symptoms, leading my friends wonder whether someone had cursed him for deserting Buddhism. Suddenly this up-and-rising former

---

* Not his real name

monk had fallen from grace—certainly among Tibetan Buddhists, but also, it seemed, even from God's.

Knowing the trials he was experiencing, I wanted to ask him about his faith. I wondered if it had weakened since becoming a Christian seemed to have brought him nothing but serious trouble. I was overjoyed by his response.

"Truth is truth," he told me, "and that truth is God who sent Jesus into the world to forgive our sins and make a way for us to have an eternal relationship with God. Circumstances don't change the truth."

I was overjoyed that Pema's faith was as strong as ever. He'd chosen to trust God regardless of his circumstances. Unfortunately, many people—even Christians—respond to life's challenges much differently. When life is difficult for us and when God says no to our prayers, we often become bitter as we question him: "Why me? Do you really love me?" I was amazed at the depth of this young Christian's faith that helped him choose a far better response.

King David chose a better way as well. For seven days, he pleaded with God for the life of his child. He fasted. He prayed face down on the floor. He cried out to God. But the child died anyway. God said no to David's prayer. Incredibly, David then got up from the ground, cleaned himself up, changed his clothes, and went to the temple to worship God. No bad attitude. No cursing God. No throwing away his faith. No bitterness. David simply accepted the Lord's answer and determined to look forward rather than backwards, trusting the Lord that his ways are best.

Recently I've been dealing with a number of "no" answers myself. In fact, it seems that over the past eight or nine years, I've heard only one of two things from God: complete silence or no. Both are hard to take and can be very discouraging.

King David chose the better response: acceptance of God's answer with a heart decision to worship God anyway. This is tough to do when we've so desired something God won't give us or do for us. But it is the only response for a victorious Christian life. I am resolute in choosing to live by faith rather than by complaining against God. Like King David, I am determined to get up from my pleading and go into God's temple to praise him.

To Ponder: Has God said no to me recently?

To Pray: Lord, usually I'm quite sure that what I want is what you want, so you'll give me whatever I ask. But you are the sovereign God and your knowledge is unsurpassed. I submit to your will and your ways and will praise you faithfully however you answer. In Jesus' name, amen.

HELPING
THE BRIDE

Helping the Bride

Theme: The Church

Bible Reading: Exodus 17:8–13; Galatians 6:2

With Bernie headmaster since 1998 of Tamagawa Seigakuin girls junior and senior high school in Tokyo, I've had the opportunity to join him on several school trips. The trip to Korea with the high school juniors has been my favorite. I particularly enjoy visiting the Korean Folk Village outside Seoul. There we learn about old-style Korean life in a kind of living museum with actors and actresses who depict the customs, dances, and daily activities of many years ago.

Once, watching a traditional Korean wedding ceremony, I was fascinated by the bride's entry. She wore a colorful Korean *hanbok*, but her face was hidden behind her upraised arms, over which another bright piece of heavy silk fabric was draped. Throughout the fifteen-minute ceremony, her arms were held in this position, whether she stood, knelt, or walked—an amazing accomplishment.

She didn't do it alone. Fortunately, she had two helpers, one on either side of her. Also dressed in traditional clothing, they had only one job: holding up the bride's elbows so that she could successfully keep her arms in proper position throughout the ceremony. What would have been impossible otherwise was possible because of her two friends.

Watching the scene, I thought of the wonderful story in Exodus where Joshua led the Israelites in fighting the Amalekites. It was a touch-and-go battle whose outcome was uncertain. As long as Moses held up his hands, the Israelites were winning, but whenever they dropped, the Amalekites took the advantage. In the end, the Israelites emerged victorious because Aaron and Hur—one on each side of Moses—held his arms up so that he could remain "steady till sunset."

Many times over our years in Japan, I've puzzled over an incident in our early days in Kobe. When the father of fellow missionaries died shortly before Christmas, our colleagues chose not to tell anyone—not even us. After finally learning the news, we were shocked they'd not shared it. They explained they'd not wanted to spoil everyone's Christmas celebrations by delivering sad news. I understood their words, but I couldn't understand their decision, especially in light of Paul's instructions in Galatians: "Carry each other's burdens, and in this way you will fulfill the law of Christ."

How can we do this if the burden isn't shared? The church is an important part of God's plan for caring for his beloved children. You and I are the church, and together, as the family of God, we are used by God to meet the needs of his people. When we don't bear each other's burdens, we thwart his plans for supplying needs and maybe even for answering prayers.

Just as the Korean bride's two friends helped carry her burden, God wants to meet our needs through brothers and sisters in Christ. Otherwise, we'd be instructed to depend upon God alone. On the contrary, the Bible is clear: we are to help the bride, the church of Jesus Christ (Isaiah, 2 Corinthians, Revelation). As I respond obediently, may I also to be a lifter of arms like Aaron and Hur. God help me.

To Ponder: How can I help the Bride?

To Pray: Lord God, here I am. Purify me and then use me to serve your church, I pray. May I never serve out of selfish ambition or pride, but only to be pleasing to you, only to lift arms so that your church may accomplish all you intend. In Jesus' name, amen.

A MOST BEAUTIFUL SOUND

Theme: Praise

Bible Reading: Deuteronomy 32:3–4; Psalm 139:13–16

*I*t wasn't always this way. I can remember sleeping pretty much across America on our nearly annual family cross-country trips from Indiana to visit grandparents in Oregon. It was a good way to pass the three days in the car, especially across flat Nebraska with its endless miles of corn and wheat fields. I could sleep anywhere, anytime, and for as long as I wanted. But that was forever ago. Today I need my own pillow and, even more importantly, an eye mask and ear plugs. Some time ago—I'm not sure when—I realized the horrible truth: I've become a delicate sleeper.

If it were only that, but it's even worse. Noises now bother me in the daytime too. Sometimes the songs of the children in the kindergarten that meets downstairs beneath our apartment are sweet—like those spring mornings when they sing,

"Saita, saita, turipu no hana ga naranda, naranda, aka, shiro, ki-iro." (This favorite song of all Japanese children translates as, "Bloomed, bloomed, the tulips have bloomed. All lined up, all lined up, red, white, and yellow.") But more often than not, there's a screamer in the bunch. His voice cuts through the sweetness like a fingernail raked across a chalkboard. I love kids—and Japanese children are some of the cutest in the world—but this one needs to be muzzled, especially when I'm facing a writing deadline.

There's also an orchestra that practices downstairs every Saturday afternoon. Actually, I think it's only a string quintet, but even one instrumentalist would irritate me because the session tends to begin just about the time I want to take a nap. Even my earplugs can't drown them out. Testing my patience even more, they practice for four hours without break!

Nevertheless, everything was different one Wednesday. "Now we're going to hear the heart beat," Dr. Sakamoto announced. And there it was: *thu-thump, thu-thump, thu-thump.* Any words I might have said were immediately caught in my throat, and my eyes filled with tears that trickled down my cheeks. Bernie, to my right, had the same reaction as we stared, transfixed, at the sonogram monitor that introduced us to our first grandbaby, scheduled to be born in Tokyo around January 31, 2008.

Three days later, I continued to be awed by the miracle of life growing inside our daughter. Remembering the high possibility that Stephanie would not be able to conceive, I could only praise God along with King David, who declared, "For you created my inmost being; you knit me together in my mother's womb. I praise you because I am fearfully and wonderfully made; your works are wonderful, I know that full well. My frame was not hidden from you when I was made in the secret place. When I was woven together in the depths of the earth, your eyes saw my unformed body. All the days ordained for me were written in your book before one of them came to be" (Psalm 139:13–16).

Thu-thump, thu-thump, thu-thump. It was a baby, alive and well, at twelve weeks and three days after conception. It was a most beautiful sound.

To Ponder: When I look at my family members, do I remember and praise God that he created them?

To Pray: Thank you, Lord, for the gift of my family. As I speak their names right now, help me to see each one as you do—as your beloved creation. Renew my love and appreciation for my family and help me find ways to express both to them. In Jesus' name, amen.

SIT STILL, MY DAUGHTER

Theme: Trust

Bible Reading: Hebrews 13:5b–6, 8; Romans 8:28, 35–39

I've never heard God's voice, but he spoke to me so clearly one day that I can describe it. It's the voice of love and compassion, of peace in the middle of a storm, the voice I will follow the rest of my life.

It was September 4, 2009. The theme verse for that day's Bible readings surprised me: "Be still, my daughter." I couldn't imagine where those words were found, so I looked up the reference: Ruth 3:18. Surely I'd read this before, but it had never spoken to me as it did after I compared this version (New King James) with the New International, the Bible translation I usually read. It declared, "Wait, my daughter ..."

Immediately I noticed the difference in feeling between the two versions. With the word *waiting*, I visualized the start of a horse race. Mounted horses wait in chutes for the buzzer to sound, the gates to bang open, the bolting forward as the race begins. Although waiting, there is no stillness. Muscles are taut with expectation, and there is impatient movement, even though controlled by the small confines of the chute and the jockey atop the horse. Amidst some pawing and tension-filled snorting, horses and riders are completely alert as they focus not on waiting but on the moment they'll be set free. There is absolutely no resting in this kind of waiting.

"Sit still, my daughter," is entirely different. I pictured sitting with my mother in church so many years ago as a child. If I jiggled my legs or swung them back and forth under the pew, she'd put her hand on my leg and say quietly, "Sit still, Cheryl." What she meant was, "Stop jiggling and be quiet. Later you can play. But for now, be still."

I also recalled her hand on my tiny, feverish forehead. "Lie still, Cheryl, and rest," she'd soothe. It didn't matter what I should have been doing, wished I were doing, or wanted to be doing. The immediate call was for stillness, through which healing would come.

After meditating on the passage, I wrote in my journal: "Stillness goes with quietness (both of body and spirit). It implies peacefulness, rest, and renewal. Father, I hear you this morning, 'Sit still, my daughter.' I will obey. I will remain quietly in this moment, not anticipating the future, just reveling in your presence."

I had no way of knowing that later that very day my respiratory doctor would tell me, "I suspect your renal cell carcinoma has returned."

At first, awaiting the results of a CT scan ordered to confirm the doctor's suspicions, I felt numb—not good, not bad, not anything. But slowly the impact of his words began invading my protective shell. Suddenly my mind was the lead NASCAR driver. No longer in that hospital waiting area, I was now racing ahead and wondering whether I'd see Christmas in December or the birth of my granddaughter in January.

With thoughts teetering on panic, I heard God's gentle, soothing voice, "Sit still, my daughter." Immediately, the tension and fear disappeared as I refocused on his presence. Circumstances had changed, even dramatically. But the One who said, "Never will I leave you; never will I forsake you," also "is the same yesterday and today and forever." And in that moment, I heard his comforting voice.

"Sit still, my daughter," he reminded me. With gratitude overflowing, I answered, "Yes, Father, I will obey."

To Ponder: Is there a circumstance in my life I'm not trusting fully to the Lord?

To Pray: You know what is weighing so heavily on my mind and heart right now, Heavenly Father. Help me to trust you completely and to believe fully "that in all things God works for the good of those who love him…" In Jesus' name, amen.

RIVERS OF DELIGHT

Theme: God's Mercy

Bible Reading: Psalm 36:5–9; Philippians 4:13

*T*hey feast on the abundance of your house; you give them drink from your river of delights. For with you is the fountain of life; in your light we see light" (Psalm 36:8–9).

It was August 2006. Sitting on the gravelly banks of the Kootenai River, outside the small town of Libby, Montana, I was captivated by the scenery before me. An evergreen-forested mountainside rose up from across the sparkling river. The stately trees appeared as if in layers, one after the other and continuing to the top, testimony to the logging and paper industries that once energized the now sleepy village.

But it was the river that held me spellbound. I could hear nothing but the roar of Kootenai Falls pounding its fury into the picturesque waterway. And yet the sound was soothing, almost hypnotizing, as I absorbed the pristine waters with my eyes.

"Remember this scene. You're going to need it when you return to Tokyo."

The voice in my heart was as clear as if I'd heard it audibly, and I startled as if I had. But that was all. Within moments I'd slipped back into my trance. Two days later, we left Montana. Thoughts of that peaceful time at the river were replaced by logistics and church speaking engagements while we continued our home assignment from Japan. (We were doing what all missionaries must do periodically in order to raise both prayer and financial support in their homelands.) I soon completely forgot the Kootenai River. Until three days after I returned to Japan.

We were changing trains in Shibuya, one of Tokyo's busiest transfer stations. Although it was Sunday morning, meaning fewer people were trying to transfer at the same time we were, the stairs, escalators, and train platforms were still packed. Our forward momentum was no quicker than if a solid line of ants had been making its way through the station. Without warning, I was irritated beyond words by all the people and I wanted to shout in my loudest voice, "GET OUT OF MY WAY!" which surely wouldn't have won any converts to Christ. I said nothing, of course, but in that moment I suddenly had no love for the life of a missionary in Tokyo.

Just as my impatience abruptly surfaced with a vengeance, I unexpectedly found myself back at the Kootenai River in my mind. And just as swiftly, I felt my spirit calming and my annoyance with the people around me dissipating. I had drunk deeply from a river of delights and now my thirsty soul was being revived once again.

How like the Lord, I contemplated later in the quiet of our apartment. He knows my weaknesses and those things with which I struggle most. But instead of condemning me, he prepares and empowers me both to face and to overcome them. Because of God's amazing grace and mercy, I testify with Paul, the greatest of all missionaries, "I can do everything through him who gives me strength."

To Ponder: What is the most difficult task or reality I am facing?

To Pray: God of amazing grace and mercy, pour these out on me today as I face what is so difficult. I am sure to fail without you. Sometimes I am so afraid of failure that I run away. Help me to remember that you are the enabler. In Jesus' name, amen.

THE TUNNEL

Theme: Trust

Bible Reading: Proverbs 3:5–8; John 16:33

Waiting is not something I do easily. Here's my secret: as long as cars aren't coming, I often walk across streets against red lights. Why wait when I can go?

Living with cancer challenges my impatience. Whether it's waiting on results of blood tests, CT scans, ultrasounds, and x-rays, waiting on doctors' appointments and prescriptions to be filled, waiting on a surgery date, or a hundred kinds of other waiting, I'm learning that the cancer journey is one of wait, wait, and wait some more.

One of the most difficult waits was in March 2009, a two-week period between first hearing of the possibility of kidney cancer and having the doctor's suspicion confirmed. How thankful I am that the Lord ministered to me during that challenging time, especially through a vision.

During that wait we prayed earnestly that cancer wouldn't be found. Yet one evening, I felt the Lord preparing me for the news no one wants to hear. It was a surprisingly comforting message, considering that I longed to be told, "No cancer." As God revealed himself to me, I envisioned a tunnel—a very long tunnel. Explicitly I knew that, while God can and does heal any way he chooses, my path to healing was not going to be a quick flight across the tree-covered mountain range towering in front of me. Instead, God was going to take me through the mountains.

Momentarily I was in a tunnel, one defying description because of the darkness. Although I should have been frightened—at least confused—by the unknown, I was strangely at peace in that unfamiliar place. When I realized I wasn't alone, I had no reason to fear. While I couldn't see him, I knew he was there and that we were walking hand in hand. At times, I would stumble as the long pathway rose and then dipped without warning, but that only caused me to grip his hand more securely. And when I suddenly squeezed tightly, he always squeezed back reassuringly, reminding me silently that although I didn't know the road, he did; I would be fine as long as I trusted him.

He also pointed out the light at the extreme far end of the tunnel. If I kept my hand in his and my eyes on the light in the distance, we would pass safely through this never-before-traveled passageway called cancer. Although I sensed that the road ahead would be long and difficult, I felt confident and assured about what was to come.

But the following September, when I heard that my cancer had returned, my shoulders slumped and my head fell forward into my hands, as if the news was too heavy a burden to bear. It was only a fleeting response to the unwelcome news.

Almost as quickly as the weariness set in, I remembered the tunnel and Jesus' comforting presence and peace. Yes, I was still in the tunnel, but my hand remained in his.

While I wasn't with the disciples when Jesus comforted these closest followers and tried to prepare them for his return to heaven, it seems I've also heard his encouraging words: "I have told you these things, so that in me you may have peace. In this world you will have trouble. But take heart! I have overcome the world" (John 16:33). In fact, I hear them often in this tunnel. I know without doubt that all is well.

To Ponder: What is the tunnel I am walking in now?

To Pray: Father, I grasp your hand today in this tunnel, admitting I am afraid of the dark. Thank you that you are here with me. When I forget this powerful truth, squeeze my hand, Lord. Remind me of your presence and restore my trust, I pray. In Jesus' name, amen.

Week THREE

Themes: *Cheerfulness, Obedience, Prayer,*
Evangelism, Missions, and Praise

ACCUSATIONS

Theme: Cheerfulness

Bible Reading: Psalm 118:24; Proverbs 15:13; 17:22

*A*ccusations. Over our thirty-plus years in Japan, I've heard Christians and Christianity accused of many things. Years ago in Saga, in the late 1970s, an Irishman stormed out of an English speech contest because Bernie was sharing his faith in Jesus Christ. Never mind that he'd obtained permission beforehand from contest organizers. Never mind that the Irishman was a judge and that his angry outburst and sudden departure left everyone shocked and embarrassed. His accusation was that Bernie didn't respect Japanese culture because he was trying to import Christianity into this Buddhist and Shinto nation.

It was a sentiment repeated by some Brits we met while hiking in the Swiss Alps a few years later. "Why don't you just appreciate the Japanese for who they are?" they asked, more politely than the Irishman. "Why do you think you have the right to force change on them?" Needless to say, we were stunned by these encounters with fellow westerners.

But we've also heard Japanese accusations. *"Katai, kusai, kurai."* Inflexible, smelly, dark—not a few Japanese have used these adjectives to describe Christians. In other words, Christians are too serious, no fun, and they make people around them feel uncomfortable. Often Jesus' words in John 14:6, "I am the way and the truth and the life. No one comes to the Father except through me," are cited as exemplifying an attitude that goes against one of the most valued Japanese character traits—not making waves so that you fit in at all costs. When one believes and follows Jesus' teachings anyway, however politely, Japanese (and perhaps others as well) may feel uncomfortable.

Although the Japanese are usually very polite, they do lash out sometimes. This was evident in comments by Katsuya Okada, then the number two man leading the ruling Democratic Party of Japan (DPJ), as reported in a fall 2009 issue of the English language *Daily Yoimuri*. I've no idea who'd stepped on his toes, but something must have happened for him to accuse Christians of being self-righteous. Lambasting the faith, Okada denounced Christianity saying Buddhism was infinitely better; even Islam was preferable.

Shortly afterwards, the news also reported other accusations, although these caused me to smile. Coming out of Breast Cancer Awareness Month (October), the article accused women involved in breast cancer's pink ribbon campaign of being too cheerful! The writer groused that Christians wearing pink ribbons, pretending they can overcome cancer with positive attitudes, are sickening and disservice people suffering from the disease. I don't know the history of the pink ribbon campaign—was it launched by a Christian, thereby inviting this attack? But in a world of grumpy, stressed people (especially with global economics as they are), I do appreciate those who are cheerful!

I can think of many far more serious accusations. Mahatma Ghandi, India's king of nonviolent resistance, was a regular Bible reader. But the diminutive Hindu once said that while he respected Jesus Christ, he could never become a Christian because so many Christians do not follow his teachings. We Christians ought to consider this accusation very carefully and personally.

But to be accused of being too cheerful? If that's the worst that's ever said of me, I hope one day I'll face this accusation. I'll respond without hesitation from the witness chair, "Guilty as charged." I trust that the broad smile on my face will be evidence enough to convict me.

To Ponder: Am I guilty of being a *"katai, kusai, kurai"* Christian?

To Pray: Oh God, teach me to laugh more, especially at myself. Help me remember that the world is watching not only what I do but also the expressions on my face. May my cheerful countenance draw others to you, I pray. In Jesus' name, amen.

ON A STREET IN AOYAMA

Theme: Obedience

Bible Reading: Matthew 25:31–46

urprise. That was my first reaction when I saw him. Not that there aren't any homeless people in Japan. Unfortunately, the numbers are growing as even large, seemingly well-to-do companies like Toyota, Canon, and Sony announce factory closings, work slow-downs, and fewer positions. One headline in early February 2009 publicized Nissan's decision to slash 20,000 jobs worldwide. Later that year, Toyota recorded the first ever fiscal year loss in the company's seventy-one year history.

In Japan, those feeling the immediate crunch of the worldwide recession are temporary workers. Although they are the lowest class of workers—the employees that are both hired and fired first—they make up one-third of Japan's labor force. Predictions were that eighty-five thousand temporary workers would lose their jobs between October 2008 and March 2009. While not all would end up in shelters or on park benches, there was no doubt that the number of homeless in Japan was on the rise.

Still, I was surprised to see the man that day—not because he was homeless, but because of his location. He wasn't keeping warm in the underground metro approaches, where men can often be found lined up head to feet, sleeping on cardboard, newspaper, or directly on the ground. Nor was he in one of the large parks in Tokyo in makeshift cardboard or tarpaulin tents. He was on a street in Aoyama, one of the most popular entertainment and fashionable shopping areas in this city, the place where Tokyo's beautiful people hang out. This man was dirty and anything but beautiful, but there he was sitting on a curb next to his raggedy suitcase. He had a cold, and I cringed to see him blowing his nose into some scraps of newspaper.

I was on my way to a meeting and was, as usual, running late. Assuming there was nothing I could do for him, I hurried on past before stopping several feet beyond to begin fishing in my purse. I'd just received a tissue package at the train station. I could give him that so at least he wouldn't have to use newspaper. I turned back, handed him the packet, and heard a grateful, "Thank you," in response.

Actually, it was an embarrassingly little thing I did. What sacrifice is there in giving away a free package of tissues? This act didn't cost me anything other than a minute of my time, at most. But there was definitely a new spring in my step as I continued on my way. I was happy I'd done something rather than just walking on by as usual. I'd been praying that God would open my eyes to needs around me and use me to touch people with little acts of kindness. I had no illusions that my tissue packet would change the man's life and that suddenly he'd get up, bathe, put on clean clothes, get a job, and become a contributing member of society. But maybe, even for an instant, he realized he is a valuable human being worthy of someone's notice in an upscale part of Tokyo.

In fact, I want to notice more. I pray that stopping on that street in Aoyama was only the start.

To Ponder: How often do I walk with my eyes truly open?

To Pray: Jesus, even as you healed the blind in Bible times, heal my own blindness today. Help me to see the people I pass on the street. Help me to notice their needs, and help me to be your hands and feet in ministering to them. In Jesus' name, amen.

BEING THERE, HERE

Theme: Prayer

Bible Reading: 2 Chronicles 7:14; James 5:13–16

*N*o doubt about it. In my generation alone, technology has dramatically changed the life of missionaries. Thanks to the computer and Skype, we're watching our grandchildren grow up even though we're separated by oceans and nations. Amazing!

During our early days in Japan, we had a two-color television (purple and green, and even those colors were iffy on the set we'd rescued from the trash); no telephone in our two-room apartment (and cell phones didn't yet exist); and a pit toilet in an attached building (today we appreciate heated toilet seats). We wrote letters by hand that reached America in seven days. If someone on the other end was an eager letter-writer (most of our friends and many family were not), it took another week for a reply. When Bernie's grandmother died unexpectedly, a telegram brought the sad news in choppy sentences written to conserve words and money while still conveying the essential message. The thought of making an international telephone call was akin to dialing the moon; it just wasn't done. Today we call our children and grandchildren even daily.

And when we do, we're rewarded with a cute little voice, "Coco? Papaw?" We may hear our grandson's names for us numerous times and with growing insistence and impatience until our computers finally get in sync. Then suddenly, when Little Ben sees our faces, his voice rises with excitement as he nearly sings, "Hiiiiiiiiiii." His longing to see us quickly satisfied, he then scoots from the chair and runs off to play.

In the meantime, our hearts have melted again. How could we be so lucky as to be there (in China) while we are here (in Japan)? We'd love to run next door for a hug—if he lived that close—but considering our experience of years ago and how wonderfully different it is today, we've no complaints about this arrangement that allows us to be there, here.

We're also rejoicing as we experience being here, there. What an incredible journey we've been on since the word *cancer* morphed from being someone else's encounter to being ours, up close and personal. We've obeyed James' instructions, "Is any one of you sick? He should call the elders of the church to pray over him and anoint him with oil in the name of the Lord. And the prayer offered in faith will make the sick person well; the Lord will raise him up" (5:14). And we've learned that people around the world also are doing the same on our behalf. Through proxies who've knelt in our place, we've continued being here as we are there, being anointed and prayed for countless times for healing.

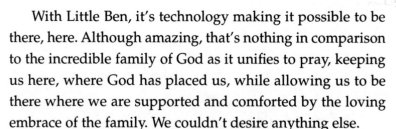

With Little Ben, it's technology making it possible to be there, here. Although amazing, that's nothing in comparison to the incredible family of God as it unifies to pray, keeping us here, where God has placed us, while allowing us to be there where we are supported and comforted by the loving embrace of the family. We couldn't desire anything else.

To Ponder: Who should I pray for today?

To Pray: Thank you for bringing to mind (a certain name), Lord. I lift him/her to you, for you have commanded prayer. Help me not to give up, even if I don't see immediate results, even if I don't see any results. I will obey your call to pray in Jesus' name. Amen.

NOT A CHANCE ENCOUNTER

Not a Chance Encounter

Theme: Evangelism, Missions

Bible Reading: Acts 8:26–40; 1 Peter 3:15

mma. I met her poolside while on vacation. We were unlikely conversation partners: she, in her mid-twenties, on her honeymoon, and holding a can of beer in her right hand while occasionally drawing on the cigarette in her left; me, enjoying the solitude and quiet of the sinking sun whose pink, red, and orange hues were gradually transforming the western sky into an exquisite palette of breathtaking beauty.

Actually, I wasn't in the mood for talking with anyone, especially one so obviously different from myself. Only a short time earlier, I'd been crying. It was the last day of our vacation, but more than that, only one week before we'd return to Japan after a three-month home assignment. (The transition back to the mission field is never easy, no matter how many times we've done it.) So the tears had come, first only a couple down my cheeks, and then suddenly a torrent shook my shoulders. Eventually the flood subsided and I went outside to be comforted by the approaching sunset—until Emma approached.

Despite my mood, I smiled back at her cheerful greeting. Sitting down on the edge of the elevated pool area, Emma struck up a conversation. Before long I was answering an oft-repeated question when someone discovers we've lived in Japan all our adult lives. "Wow!" Emma marveled at our tenure, telling me that she was only twenty-six years old herself. "You must have been really young when you went. Wasn't that scary?"

"When you're young, you never imagine there's something you can't do," I replied with a laugh, even as a voice inside told me not to miss this opportunity to share the real reason we went to Japan. It wasn't just that we were young—I was twenty-one and Bernie twenty-two—and looking for adventure; the main reason was God's call upon our lives. "Actually, we're Christian missionaries," I told Emma. "That's why we went to Japan and have stayed so long."

As I expected, there was a momentary pause in the conversation as if Emma was wondering what she'd gotten herself into and evaluating whether to go any further. To my surprise, she proceeded to tell me that she is an agnostic who wonders whether atheists just might be right about the nonexistence of God. Nevertheless, she is very curious about religion and has her own repertoire of religious experiences, including infant baptism in the Lutheran church and rebaptism in a Pentecostal church as a teenager.

What in the world can I say that will make any difference to Emma? I prayed silently as we conversed. In the end, I shared with my new friend that knowing God is not about religion but about relationship. I urged her to continue keeping her ears open because God so desires an intimate relationship that he is pursing her, even through our talk. I also told her I appreciated our conversation after she thanked me for not judging her.

"It was a gift to me," I assured her. Noting the quizzical expression on her face, I added, "It's been a tough day, but the God I believe in and trust just used you to encourage me."

Whether or not Emma could understand, I have no doubt that this was not a chance encounter. Through a confused agnostic, God reminded me of his desire to use me as his hands, feet, listening ears, and heart—even on vacation. And most especially in Japan.

To Ponder: What chance encounter has God sent my way?

To Pray: I am willing, Lord God, to be your hands, feet, ears, and heart for those around me who are confused about you. Help me to be aware of others seeking you, so that when they ask the reason for the hope I have, I'll always be prepared with my answer. In Jesus' name, amen.

ON AGING

On Aging

Theme: Praise

Bible Reading: Psalm 71:17–23; Hebrews 13:8

ernie and I clinked our new glasses together one morning, but it wasn't a toast. In fact, they weren't drinking glasses that touched, but eye glasses. We always pray together at the start of the day, kiss, and then go our separate ways. But when we'd kissed that morning, our glasses clinked and we laughed about how things are changing. There's no denying the aging process.

But sometimes it is shocking. I clearly remember an incident that occurred when I was thirty-six years old. Operation Mobilization was seeking volunteers to help when its ship, the *Doulos*, docked in Kobe. We were living there then and I was excited to serve—until I heard they wanted volunteers between the ages of eighteen and thirty-five. I was shocked to be too old! That was the first time I'd ever thought about aging. I seem to think about it a lot these days, and all the more since a co-worker said she feels comfortable at our house because our dinnerware is the same pattern her grandparents have. (I'd heard this pattern is now found only in antique stores, but I'd not considered the implications.)

Then I suffered another shock at our gym when the athletic trainer-to-be suddenly announced, "*Shitsureishimasu*." Roughly translated as, "Excuse my rudeness," these words are a hallmark of Japan's traditionally genteel manners, making it possible for people to get along even in one of the most crowded nations in the world. Perhaps times are changing.

Before I had a chance to respond or understand what she really meant, she grabbed my right hip in her hand and squeezed it firmly. To my horror, she then declared loudly enough for everyone in the room to hear, "Just as I thought! You hips are sagging!"

Recovering slightly, I joked back, "At this age, everything is sagging!"

To which she responded without the slightest hint of jest, "Hmmm," meaning—not very subtly—"I agree entirely." I was joking; she wasn't, not even a bit.

There it was—a one-word evaluation of my physique at fifty-two years of age: sagging. Whether it's the bags under my eyes that exceed the allowable size for airplane carry on pieces, the soft undersides of my arms that wave like flags in the wind, or other less noticeable (when fully clothed) areas of my body, the word with which I was branded is as specific and accurate as nutrition fact labels on food products. But then again, we'd joined the gym because we did indeed hope to shape up.

Sagging. And to think there was a time when one of my biggest worries was how my mini-skirt or striped bell bottoms looked on my still slim legs and how my floppy suede hat appeared on my straight, back-length, yet-uncolored brown hair. (Yes, I was coming of age in the late 1960s.) Reading this morning's headlines—terrorism, a faltering worldwide economy, and much more—I thought about how times and appearances, and worries, have changed.

In this day of change, I am so glad that, "Jesus Christ is the same yesterday and today and forever." He is the one constant on whom I can depend.

To Ponder: The changeless God is always worthy of praise.

To Pray: I will always praise you, Lord God, even on days I wish I were younger. To be sure, many things in my life have changed, but you have not and will not. How I praise your consistency, your faithfulness, your abiding presence in my life! In Jesus' name, amen.

YET I WILL REJOICE

Theme: Praise

Bible Reading: Habakkuk 3:16–19; Philippians 4:4–7

*M*aybe she had never been so afraid in her short life-time as when the stranger suddenly appeared. Not only had her home been invaded, but the unknown white woman (me) in the infant's mostly ebony world was lurking behind a black camera, coming too close for comfort in preparing to take the photo. The many holes in the little girl's threadbare red shirt, the rough board hut behind her that could not keep out the chicks and other much more worrisome creatures, and the hard-packed, dry dirt ground on which she sat all spoke with exclamation marks of the poverty of Tanzania, her homeland.

There's much one can fear in the world, even one as young as she. Not yet speaking or even standing, she certainly had no ability to defend herself against poverty, malnutrition, AIDS and other diseases, genocide and war, and other horrors she knew nothing about—yet. In time, they are likely to become the harsh and unwelcome realities of her life. These too will bring tears.

How different the reaction when her mother appeared! Although a tear still rolled down her tender cheek, a confident smile now lit up her face. From fright to freedom, from tears to triumph—all because she knew her mother. I was still there. So was the poverty and everything else that challenged the daily life of her family. Nothing had changed, except that her mother was now visible. And with her mother's presence, peace, joy, and hope were restored.

What a perfect picture of the way it can be as we relate to our heavenly Father. When we know him, when we understand and believe in the very core of our beings his promise that he is always present with us and will never leave us, we can rejoice no matter what the circumstances.

The Old Testament prophet Habakkuk knew this intimately. It was why, in spite of being so afraid that he admitted that his heart pounded and his lips quivered, he confidently declared, "Though the fig tree does not bud and there are no grapes on the vines, though the olive crop fails and the fields produce no food, though there are no sheep in the pen and no cattle in the stalls, yet I will rejoice in the LORD, I will be joyful in God my Savior."

Many times during my cancer journey I have recalled Habakkuk's astounding words of praise and this incident from a visit to Tanzania in 1992. I, too, declare that I will rejoice in the Lord—no matter what a medical test reveals or a doctor tells me, no matter the length of the journey nor its eventual outcome, no matter what.

"Be strong and courageous," God told Joshua, preparing to lead the children of Israel. "Do not be terrified; do not be discouraged, for the LORD your God will be with you wherever you go" (Joshua 1:9). And with my Father's presence, peace, joy, and hope are always restored.

To Ponder: What fear in my life could I conquer through praising God?

To Pray: I need your help, Heavenly Father, to give my fear to you. Maybe I will need to give it to you many times as I fight this battle against fear. I praise you even before the victory because you are the faithful God who always answers when we pray in Jesus' name. Amen.

A HAUNTING VISION

Theme: Evangelism, Missions

Bible Reading: Acts 20:17–24; 2 Timothy 4:1–8

The crisp temperatures were perfect for camping. While on an afternoon hike, we'd already enjoyed the palette of fall colors God had splashed throughout the trees. Then the sun set, serenely washing the sky in pinks, oranges, and blues. Now a full harvest moon illuminated the night sky.

All the breathtaking imagery of a perfect October evening in Indiana was heightened as I glanced over at Bernie, tending the campfire in his cowboy hat, denim shirt, and jeans. Leisurely pouring himself a cup of coffee, he looked so different from the man I usually see in Tokyo, whose schedule finds him running from meeting to meeting, always clad in dress shirt, necktie, and suit, often pressured because the expectations are far greater than can possibly be accomplished by one man in one lifetime. Nevertheless, he tries, and the resulting tiredness is as evident as his blue eyes and mustached upper lip. But I saw none of that around the campfire. The real Bernie had returned, and his satisfaction was as soothing as the hot cup of coffee he soon sipped in silence.

Shortly afterwards, I met another blue-eyed, mustached gentleman. A generation older than my husband, he obviously suffered from Parkinson's disease and the inevitable physical decline that comes with more than eight decades of life. Nevertheless, this descendent of Scandinavian forefathers had recently become pastor of a church—not an interim pastor, but the full-time leader. Granted, the congregation was small, but helping people is never a small task. And at his age and condition? It was not the peaceful image of an evening around a campfire.

Neither was the toddler's hand that grasped at the unyielding padlock that held an old wooden door tightly shut in a rural Indian village. No matter how her chubby little fingers worked at it, no matter how many times she tugged at it, the square silver lock obstinately refused to give in and open. Consequently, the door remained closed to her.

But that's as it should be. One cannot fault a padlock for doing its job. Yet I'm haunted by that vision from a trip to India in 2008. The tiny, milk chocolate–colored hand on that lock paints the picture of the difficulty of sharing Jesus Christ in so many parts of the world, Japan included. Who will introduce the key to the uncompromising locks that bind so much of our world today?

Jesus declared, "Here I am! I stand at the door and knock. If anyone hears my voice and opens the door, I will come in and eat with him, and he with me" (Revelation 3:20). But who would quickly open a door to a stranger? Not many people.

Yet we'd all warmly welcome our friends. I'd like to be that friend, bringing Jesus along with me as I visit. It can't be left to eighty-something-year-old people in ill health alone, no matter how willing they may be. Where are the others who will join me in this mission? Where are the ones who will come after me?

To Ponder: I am holding the key to life for someone. Who is he or she?

To Pray: Lord, I praise you for salvation and eternal life. But your gifts are not for me alone. You have called me to share them with others. I cannot be silent and satisfied when so many people have never heard your good news. Empower me, I pray. In Jesus' name, amen.

Week FOUR

Themes: *Praise, Forgiveness, Faith,*
The Tongue, God's Faithfulness,
and Obedience

IN HIS ARMS

Theme: Praise

Bible Reading: Psalm 42:1–2, 11; 43:3–5

"Praise the Lord; praise God our Savior!
For each day he carries us in his arms" (Psalm 68:19 NLT).

I doubt I've ever felt so alone in my whole life.

There I was in one of Moscow's domestic airports, awaiting a flight to the Ural Mountain region. A young Russian lawyer had delivered me there, offering to wait and make sure I had no problems checking in. But I already felt I'd taken enough of his time. Besides, I'd traveled considerably in many countries of the world. I'd be fine, so I thanked him and sent him on his way.

Big mistake. Seasoned traveler or not, this airport was unlike any I'd visited previously. Dark and dingy, its disconcerting interior wasn't my only problem. My biggest challenge was the Russian language. I didn't know it, and no one around me spoke English. Nor were signs written in anything other than Cyrillic script. I didn't know where to go, what to do, or whom to ask, and there were no volunteers to take my hand and lead me through the mostly deserted building that was as unwelcoming as an empty warehouse.

As a sudden tiredness enveloped me, I sat down on a hard bench in what was, I assumed, a waiting room. At least I was waiting there. The wall in front of me was covered with what appeared to be advertising posters of all sizes and shapes. Not one made any sense to me, and the busyness of the wall exhausted me all the more, exacerbating my loneliness. I have never felt so alone in my life.

It was then I noticed a tiny sign buried in the middle of that tempestuous sea of Cyrillic. Two little English words stood out in dramatic contrast and announced: God cares. Unexpectedly, everything was different. I was still confused and in an unfamiliar location, but I'd been reminded of an important truth: God was there too. Surely he would carry me in his arms until I was safely at my destination.

Sometimes living with cancer is lonely too.

One year into my cancer journey as I was walking from the hospital to the train station, the Lord reminded me once again that he is worthy of praise—no matter what. It was a gentle reminder, but pointed nevertheless. The news from the doctor hadn't been good since the latest CT scan showed that the tumor growing in the vacuum where my left kidney had been was now even bigger. It seemed the medicine was no longer effectively fighting the cancer that had recurred.

I'd have preferred different news. But in the short five-minute walk to the train station, the Lord reminded me that he is yet God, yet in control, yet omniscient, yet omnipresent, and still the same yesterday, today, and forever. He reminded me that he is still carrying me in his arms and most worthy of praise. I recalled my decision of years ago to praise him in all circumstances and I determined once again to obey.

To Ponder: How is my praise life?

To Pray: Lord, I'm struggling today with a heavy feeling. I can't describe it, but it's real nevertheless. Thank you for understanding and accepting my feelings. Thank you that you will help me overcome as I praise you for who you are. No matter what, you are worthy of praise. In Jesus' name, amen.

THREE STRIKES, I'M OUT!

Three Strikes, I'm Out!

Theme: Forgiveness

Bible Reading: Job 2:7–10; Psalm 19:14

*I*t wasn't until evening that I struck out that Thursday. I'd endured a jam-packed commuter train first thing in the morning. Such trains are perhaps the part of Tokyo living I detest most. But if I wanted to make my appointment, I had to ride the train. Fortunately, I was able to wiggle into the middle of the car to find breathing space. Also the person closest to my face sported a mask, for which I thanked him silently, grateful to be spared his germs. Despite the crowd, I was feeling fine when the train arrived in Shibuya.

But then came the bank. Actually, it's a tossup as to which I loathe more: commuter trains or Japanese banks. But still I was feeling good—until a new teller called my name. I handed her my properly endorsed check and driver's license and told her my business, adding, "I come here every month and do the same thing every month." To which she replied, "Do you have an account at this bank?" "Yes, look at the check, please. I come here every month for the same business." I was getting a little annoyed. Smiling, but still looking puzzled, she thanked me and asked me to wait while she processed my check.

No sooner had I sat down than she called me back. Which was my first name: Cheryl, Ann, or Barton? "It's just as it's written here on the check I want to cash, the same business I do here every month," I responded. "And how do you pronounce these names?" she asked. "What difference does it make?" I wanted to reply, but didn't. After her English pronunciation lesson, she invited me to sit down again.

A second later, she called me yet again. Now she asked how my name is written in *katakana*, a Japanese phonetic alphabet used for foreign words. When I protested that I do this every month and with the same driver's license (no katakana) and an identical check written to me from our account (no katakana), she continued, "Well, don't you have something in katakana?" By now I was beyond annoyance and wasn't about to admit I did have katakana identification. Instead, I replied, "Every month I show my driver's license," which is true. Finally, she gave up and cashed my check—the same way it's done every month. Swallowing my irritation, I left the bank smiling that I'd not have to return for a month.

The rest of the day went well until Bernie and I, walking to an evening meeting, came upon a woman pushing a stroller on the roadside. There were no sidewalks or pedestrian shoulders, so a line of cars was forming behind her. Finally, I decided to pass. Fully expecting a cute baby in the buggy, I was shocked to discover two cats instead. Irritation that apparently had been building all day suddenly boiled over as I ranted about how she was holding up traffic—and us—with CATS!

"Three strikes, I'm out!" I thought to myself later. That very morning I'd been memorizing Philippians 4:8: "Finally, brothers, whatever is true, whatever is noble, whatever is right, whatever is pure, whatever is lovely, whatever is admirable—if anything is excellent or praiseworthy—think about such things." How badly I'd failed to implement these words. Instead, it seemed, I could only complain.

To Ponder: Have I failed God recently?

To Pray: Jesus, although Peter denied you three times, you forgave him anyway. When I fail miserably—three times or thirty—please forgive me also. "May the words of my mouth and the meditation of my heart be pleasing in your sight, O Lord," I pray. In Jesus' name, amen.

WAITING ON APPLES

Waiting on Apples

Theme: Faith

Bible Reading: Mark 11:22–24; Hebrews 11:1, 6

*B*eing a top student was always important to me in school. If I wasn't going to win awards for my athletic prowess, my musical abilities, or my inventive genius, at least I could stand tall when grades were handed out. And I did.

Which is why it's such a surprise that I'm so slow in learning some of life's most important lessons—not the ABCs, but far more valuable things like faith, patience, and perseverance. The Lord, using my two-year-old grandson, is determined I have every opportunity to catch up where I'm behind in my lessons.

"Coco, how're ya' feeling?" Little Ben asked as he walked into my bedroom where I was sitting, exhausted, in a chair.

"Not so good," I responded, adding, "That's why Coco's a little sad today."

Without missing a beat and with all the certainty of an experienced and learned elder, Benjamin continued, "Jesus will help you."

Smiling at my grandson for reminding me of such a fundamental truth, I hugged him and said, "You're absolutely right! Jesus will help Coco feel better so I don't have to be sad."

"That's awesome!" Benjamin returned. I wanted to hug him again, but he giggled, escaped my reach, and ran out of the room. End of the lesson, but I suddenly realized I'd been left with a warm glow that had uplifted both my sad spirit and my tired body. I knew God himself had visited to restore my trust in him and his unconditional love and perfect plan for my life.

A few days later, it was time for another lesson. Benjamin and I discovered an apple tree at the back of the apartment complex where our families were spending the summer—and it was loaded with fruit. Benjamin wanted to begin eating immediately, but I explained that the apples were still mostly green; it was too soon to pick them.

"Well, let's wait," he replied matter-of-factly. "Till the apples turn red."

"But that happens little by little," I protested. To which Benjamin responded without the slightest bit of frustration as he sat down on the concrete parking block in front of the tree, "Little by little. We can wait."

How long will you wait? I wondered to myself as I sat down beside him, facing the tree and its not-going-to-be-red-for-a-long-time apples. What patience! More than that, what trust! With little concept of time, my grandson was willing to sit and wait expectantly simply because he believed me when I told him the apples will turn red eventually. No doubts in his mind that what I said was true—just because I said so.

"Now faith is being sure of what we hope for and certain of what we do not see," (Hebrews 11:1). I think of God's promises of healing and answered prayer. I realize again that I need to sit quietly more often—even on a parking block—and wait patiently for the Lord to fulfill his words. If my grandson can do it, why can't I?

To Ponder: Do I really believe God answers my prayers?

To Pray: Father, it's no wonder Jesus said we must become like little children to enter the kingdom of heaven. Children have such wonderful faith! May I be more childlike in mine, I pray. Teach me to trust you more as I wait patiently on you to answer. In Jesus' name, amen.

LAUGHTER, THE BEST MEDICINE

Theme: The Tongue

Bible Reading: Proverbs 12:18; 15:1–4

etter to laugh than cry, says I." It was the motto Naomi and I tried to remember as we worked together as resident assistants in a freshman dorm during our junior year of college. It seemed like our floor of girls had more than its share of problems, taxing both our wisdom and relational skills. The girls and their challenges threatened our emotional well being too. The phrase was Naomi's brainchild, and it helped return smiles to our faces and laughter to our hearts (if not our lips), even in the most trying of times.

If I didn't have cancer, I might say that my urologist can be one of my biggest trials these days. Don't misunderstand me—he's a skilled doctor and I am very grateful for his care. But bedside manner? That he is lacking in this department is an understatement of classic proportions.

Take, for example, the day in March 2009 when he discussed surgery options. If he removed my kidney through laparoscopy, the surgical trauma would be minimized because he'd be working through four holes in my left side. (Pardon my simplifying things so greatly.) If I elected open surgery, he'd be able to see better (no use of monitors) and, if there was any excessive bleeding, it could be dealt with more easily and quickly. The down side, however, would be a longer recovery time and more unsightly scarring—not that I wore a bikini and had any reason to care anyway. I chose the more difficult procedure as I considered a swifter recovery.

"That's good," my doctor agreed with my decision. "I'm not sure I could cut through all your belly fat if you'd chosen open surgery."

I was too stunned—and embarrassed—by his words to retort, though many not-too-nice thoughts about his lack of bedside manner crowded my head. I'm sure I also shot a few daggers with my eyes.

They must have missed him, though, because his bedside manner never improved. Another verbal faux pas came as I was discussing my rising blood pressure. According to the literature on Sutent, my anti-cancer drug at the time, heart stress is a common side effect—which makes you wonder why this doctor had never once taken my blood pressure or even asked about it during that year! (He'd also never checked my weight, although given his comment about my inordinate belly fat, that was probably good.)

In any case, I reported to my doctor that my blood pressure had risen into the 150–165 range on top, with the bottom number in the 100–110 range. With hardly a flicker of interest, he assured me that this wasn't dangerous yet. "Besides," he added nonchalantly, "elderly people tend to have higher blood pressure anyway."

After a year of experiencing his limited bedside manner, I was ready for this jolt to my self-esteem. "Doctor," I responded emphatically, "I am NOT elderly!" "Oh, excuse me," he mumbled in reply. Although his sincerity was questionable, I let it go, covering my bemusement with laughter.

To Ponder: How could my words encourage someone today?

To Pray: Forgive me, Lord, for the careless and hurtful words that slip out of my mouth so easily. Help me to think before I speak. Cleanse my tongue and use it for your good. Send me to speak your encouraging words to someone today, I pray. In Jesus' name, amen.

THE DREAM

The Dream

Theme: God's Faithfulness

Bible Reading: Isaiah 40:28–31; Lamentations 3:22–23

I didn't know where I was or who was with me, but they were clear—the woman and her two children. "May I talk with you?" she asked, indicating with a slight nod of her head that we could go into the other room for privacy.

"I need a friend," she whispered in a voice choked with tears. It was almost as if her admission shamed her, yet she continued, "Will you be my friend?"

My heart, overwhelmed with compassion for this unknown woman, propelled me into her arms. Now tears dampened my own cheeks. "I need a friend too," I confessed, suddenly overcome with loneliness, sadness, and my own neediness. "Will you be my friend?"

Then the dream was over. I didn't recall the scene until the next evening when I suddenly shared it with my family.

Once again my eyes welled and overflowed in two streams down my face.

What do dreams mean? I'm not an interpreter, nor do I think it's useful to dwell on these partial scenes that fill the nighttime and occasionally spill over into the day. But I'd become a prisoner to the loneliness that permeated that dream. It lingered, not as the fragrance of a lovely scented candle after being extinguished, but like a persistent headache threatening to explode into a debilitating migraine.

In the quietness of the darkened room as I patted my newborn granddaughter to sleep that night, the Lord came to me in my thoughts and reminded me not of a dream but of reality. "My child, have I not promised never to leave you?" he asked in the most loving voice I've ever heard. "Why are you so lonely?"

One after another, God then recapped the significant ways he'd been present in the preceding few days: through e-mails reminding us of prayers; lunch at the home of a friend who greeted me, "You're looking wonderful!" after I'd noticed the unsmiling, tired, unexpectedly old face staring back at me from the mirror; surprising gifts that had arrived to help ease the financial burdens of the cancer journey; the visit of good friends who, although very busy, wanted to say in person, "We're thinking of you."

And then snatches of Scripture came to mind. Although I couldn't recall them fully, enough pieces were there to be woven into a loosely knit shawl that wrapped itself around my shoulders and swaddled me lovingly in comfort. In that embrace, I prayed for three-week-old Hosanna to sleep well that night.

The next morning, I found the rest of the message that had so consoled me:

Do you not know? Have you not heard? The LORD is the everlasting God, the Creator of the ends of the earth. He will not grow tired or weary, and his understanding no one can fathom. He gives strength to the weary and increases the power of the weak. Even youths grow tired and weary, and young men stumble and fall; but those who hope in the LORD will renew their strength. They will soar on wings like eagles; they will run and not grow weary, they will walk and not be faint. (Isaiah 40:28–31)

And I? The loneliness had vanished like a dream at the first hint of dawn. Once again, God had proven his faithfulness.

To Ponder: How has God shown me his faithfulness this week?

To Pray: Oh faithful God! How I praise you! How could I ever doubt you? Yet I confess that far too often I sink into loneliness, sadness, and neediness because I have forgotten your faithfulness. Help me to see whenever you reveal yourself to me, I pray. In Jesus' name, amen.

A CHRISTMAS PRAYER

A Christmas Prayer

Theme: Obedience

Bible Reading: Luke 1:26–38

s much as I tried, I wasn't keeping up with everything I needed to do before Christmas. In fact, the to-do list only seemed to be getting longer. On top of this, our nearly two-year-old grandson and his mother had arrived early for Christmas because she was due to deliver our granddaughter in a month. Need I say more?

Every time I sat down at the computer, my little shadow came calling. "Coco, book," he'd say, pulling on my hand and meaning, "Read to me, Coco." Or, "Coco, blocks." Translated, "Let's play together with blocks." Or, "Coco, kick soccer ball." Or any number of other invitations—actually quite persistent summons to spend time with him. I was completely defenseless, pressing work or not. After all, how long would he actually want to spend time with me? And how many chances would I have to devote myself to him? I realized that if I missed these opportunities with Little Ben, I was never guaranteed others in the future. It was then or, perhaps, never.

As we played together, I was reminded of a book of daily meditations I'd been reading that Advent season. Of those I'd read, "To Be a Virgin," by Loretta Ross-Gotta, was the most thought-provoking. Bernie and I were to celebrate Christmas with our son, daughter, grandson, and other family members. We also looked forward to our thirty-fourth wedding anniversary in January. How could I be a virgin, as the author suggests both men and women must be if we will truly prepare our hearts for Christmas?

Ross-Gotta writes, "The intensity and strain that many of us bring to Christmas must suggest to some onlookers that, on the whole, Christians do not seem to have gotten the point of [Christmas]. Probably few of us have the faith or the nerve to tamper with hallowed Christmas traditions on a large scale, or with our other holiday celebrations. But a small experiment might prove interesting. What if, instead of *doing* something, we were to *be* something special? Be a womb. Be a dwelling for God. Be surprised."*

The Virgin Mary made herself available to God for his purposes (to be the mother of God's Son) when she responded to the angel, "I am the Lord's servant. May it be to me as you have said." In her case, she literally was a womb for God. For myself, I realized that I could be a womb in another way—by putting away my to-do list and offering myself to God for his use, not only in the Christmas season, but also in the coming year.

---

* Loretta Ross-Gotta, "To Be a Virgin," in *Watch for the Light*, 101 (Farmington, PA: The Plough Publishing House, 2001).

Just as my heart melts whenever my grandson, in his irresistible way, invites me to play, may it also respond passionately whenever God comes, as he did to Mary, and says, "I need you." May I never hesitate to obey from a heart of love for his gift of Jesus: babe in a manger, Savior on a cross, and the way to eternal life forever with the Father. Amen.

To Ponder: Practically speaking, how could I be a womb for God?

To Pray: Here I am, Lord God. I offer myself to you humbly for I am an unworthy vessel. More than anyone else, I know my shortcomings and failures. But I am available to you for your purposes, Father. I relinquish my short-sighted plans to yours that touch eternity. In Jesus' name, amen.

WHEN FAITH GOES ON TRIAL

Theme: Faith

Bible Reading: 2 Corinthians 4:16–18; Ephesians 2:8–10

eptember used to be one of my favorite months. Notice the past tense.

When I was a child, September meant the start of school. I looked forward to new clothes, a new lunch box, and meeting friends again for the new school year. September always spelled new and exciting to me.

But that was years ago. These days I'm thinking it might be good just to jump from August right into October—at least if the last two Septembers are indicative of what the month will hold for me in the future.

In early September 2009, I learned my cancer had recurred. Then while waiting to hear which course of treatment would be recommended, I found myself shadowboxing with fear, an opponent definitely present even if invisible. In our sparring, I also discovered many opportunities to doubt God and his good plans for my life. I'm grateful that I emerged from that month stronger in faith, but I was not without battle scars.

I remember one day in particular. Attending a fall festival, I knew my fever was going up, but I couldn't leave early. In staying, I met an acquaintance who offered to introduce me to a faith healer. The Bible teaches that God heals; it instructs us to pray for healing; and I believe God can and does heal—even miraculously, even cancer. There shouldn't have been any problems.

But then my Japanese Christian friend lowered her voice to tell me the faith healer was Buddhist. Perhaps noting my surprise, she added quickly, "But that's okay. We believe in the same God." What are you saying? I wanted to shout incredulously. Instead, I accepted the healer's calling card. Yet as the day passed, I sensed I'd carried evil home with me through that card. That evening, Bernie burned it and we prayed together for God's protection. As we did, peace returned to my troubled heart and my high fever broke. Even now, more than a year later, I'm convinced my faith was on trial that day.

September 2010. A new trial, but more subtle. After six relatively healthy weeks, my oasis in the cancer journey has ended, at least for now. Fatigue has returned and, more recently, pain accompanies it. Other symptoms hint the cancer may be more active again. All of this comes after writing a victorious blog early in September about the wonderful lessons God has taught me since my cancer recurred. Those lessons remain true as ever, but it is harder to share them as doubts assail once again. The trial is not over.

Contemplating the month, I remember a radio program I listened to recently. Being interviewed was Walter Wangerin, a Lutheran minister, university professor, and prolific author who is walking his own cancer journey. I recall his comments about cancer (and suffering) being a proving ground for faith, an opportunity like none other for faith to hold one securely in the midst of the battle. His words resounded with me then, when my faith wasn't on trial, and especially now that it is.

How long will the current trial last? I don't know. But I believe, like Wangerin, that my faith will see me through whatever comes. Mind you, this is not because my faith is extraordinary. I know the truth of Paul's words, "For it is by grace you have been saved, through faith—and this not from yourselves, it is the gift of God—not by works, so that no one can boast" (Ephesians 2:8–10), and I thank God for his amazing provision that supports my hands and feet, even when they tremble.

To Ponder: How does my faith compare to the size of a mustard seed?

To Pray: Jesus, you've said that faith the size of a tiny mustard seed is all I need. I know I have that much faith, Lord, because you gave it to me. But I confess that sometimes it wavers. In those times, please strengthen my faith and glorify yourself. In Jesus' name, amen.

Week FIVE

Themes: *Evangelism, Missions, God's Love, and Praise*

THREE WOMEN

Theme: Evangelism, Missions

Bible Reading: Luke 1:26–38

*B*oth my grandmothers have been gone for years. Yet I often remember them and wish we could sit down and chat—over chocolate chip cookies that they loved to bake (and I loved to eat). One fall, I felt I had that chance, but without cookies.

While visiting Kobe, we drove into the countryside to our favorite pottery village, Tachikui. En route, we were drawn to a thatched roof, traditional Japanese home. It always spelled character from afar, though we'd never driven up the narrow road to look closer. But this time, spontaneity took precedence over schedule. We were greeted by an older woman in customary farmer-style clothing. Her immediate smile lit up her weathered face, assuring our welcome. Her husband, also appropriately dressed, underscored the warm reception by inviting us inside to see their 260-year-old home and the woodblock prints he carves. Feigning shock that he would show off "that dirty old house," his wife delighted us with cute giggles and a lot of conversation we didn't always understand. We left with their calls to come again ringing in our ears, just as if I'd been at Grandma's house.

But the mood at Tachikui was somber when we asked about our eighty-three-year-old potter friend. He'd passed away only three weeks earlier. When his wife, back bent low by osteoporosis, came outside to greet us, I immediately embraced her and shared her tears. Both of my grandfathers died first. Once again, I felt as if I'd been with my grandmothers, comforting them in their sadness and loss.

Two days later, I visited another woman in the hospital. Although chemotherapy was causing her hair to fall out, her face remained beautiful, accented with warmth, love, and a quick smile. I tried to excuse myself after an hour, but she wanted to talk more, so I stayed. But eventually I did have to leave. Grams never wanted me to leave either. As the hospital elevator doors closed, my last glimpse was of Baaba waving. I could see Grams in her face, bringing a smile to my own.

Afterwards, however, I struggled with bittersweet feelings as I remembered these three women. As a Christian missionary, it's my fervent prayer that my Japanese friends and acquaintances come to believe that Jesus is God's Son, sent into our world to demonstrate God's love and offer forgiveness. How I long to see them open their hearts and accept the gift. But these three women, all in their eighties, are completely bound by Japanese traditions, customs, and religions, whether they believe them or not. Baaba once told us that belief is irrelevant. She'd accepted her role and its responsibilities when she married, and she would do what was expected of her until she dies. In moments of reflection, I confess that it seems impossible for any of these women—dare I say most of Japan—to come to Christ.

Although I don't understand how it's possible, I'm comforted by the angel's words to Mary: "For nothing is impossible with God." It's the only thing that keeps me going.

To Ponder: Who could I introduce to Jesus today?

To Pray: Lord, I know you want me to share your good news with others. Why am I so afraid and tongue-tied? Please calm my fears and give me your words so that my family, friends, indeed Japan and the world, may come to know you, I pray. In Jesus' name, amen.

IMMANUEL

Theme: God's Love

Bible Reading: Matthew 1:18–25; Hebrews 11:1, 6

everal years ago, while on a writing assignment in Chiang Mai, Thailand, I visited an international church during the Advent season. Although the graceful palm trees, deep pink bougainvilleas, and warm, if not hot, temperatures challenged my expectations of the backdrop necessary for Christmas, the story I heard that day was the very essence of the true meaning of Christmas. It was shared by a guest preacher, a missionary working among Thailand's tribal peoples.

Shortly beforehand, the missionary had traveled to a remote district to visit contacts that had been made in earlier trips there. This time, his young son—perhaps three or four years old—had accompanied him. Unfortunately, the boy had tripped and fallen as he walked alongside his father, and the resulting cut on his face was deep and required stitches. Although the missionary quickly located a primitive medical clinic, no anesthesia was available there—only the suturing materials. Despite the awful pain he knew would be inflicted on his son, the father agreed to the procedure anyway. Without it, the lad could risk serious infection and be disfigured for life.

"Daddy! Daddy!" the little boy shrieked in pain and terror as the clinician somehow managed to stitch the wound as his father pressed his muscular torso across the boy's body to keep him still on the examining table. "Stop! Why are you doing this to me?"

How could the father possibly explain to him so he could understand that it was out of his deep love for his firstborn that he was allowing the pain—even participating in it? He couldn't. Instead, his sobs shook his bulky frame and his tears wet the boy's soft skin beneath him.

"Oh, my son, my son," the missionary exhaled, each word a sob.

"If you only knew how much I love you. If you could only understand that I am holding you now in love, even allowing this pain because I love you. You simply can't understand, my beloved boy. But know this: I'll not leave you alone in your pain," he repeated again and again in his heart.

Even the sound of his father's voice, intended to soothe, only seemed to antagonize the boy—when he could hear it over his wailing. "If you love me, if you care, why don't you stop?" the screams seemed to accuse. "You could stop this all in an instant."

So the father, out of boundless, matchless, incomprehensible, even unrequited love, silently enveloped the writhing, agonizing body of his toddler until the horrific time finally passed. It was a big chance he took on the outcome—not whether the outward scar would heal, but whether the far more painful, costly, and dangerous scars to the heart would ever mend. He couldn't help but wonder; still his faith was even stronger than this doubt that the boy would emerge knowing, without question, the truth of the father's never-ending love for him. And on this unshakable truth, the boy would live out all the days of his life as God had ordained each one of them to be.

"The virgin will be with child and will give birth to a son, and they will call him Immanuel—which means 'God with us'" (Matthew 1:23). It is a Christmas message, to be sure. But it is more than this. It is a message to guide us throughout all the years of our lives: in love, God with us—always, forever, no matter what.

To Ponder: Through whom or in what ways did I meet Immanuel today?

To Pray: Father, there are many times I fail to recognize you in the daily experiences of life—especially in those difficult times when it is impossible to understand how the God of love could allow such pain. Strengthen my faith so that I may be sure of what I hope for and certain of what I do not see. In Jesus' name, amen.

FOR THIS
I HAVE JESUS

For This I Have Jesus

Theme: Praise

Bible Reading: Psalm 66:1–15

*I*f I were caught up on my daily Bible readings, I wouldn't have encountered today's passage from Psalm 66:1–15. (I should have read this more than a week ago.) But because I *am* behind, I read verses about praising God and telling others of all he has done for me. It was exactly what I needed. Instead of dwelling in the land of no motivation, no energy, no enthusiasm, and a whole bunch of other negatives, I was reminded again this morning that the key to unlocking the door of this cruel prison that has ensnared me is to focus not on cancer (nor on yet another gray, rainy day) but on praising God for who he is.

The accompanying devotional piece was not lengthy—only five very short paragraphs—but they packed a tremendously powerful punch at the very place where my heart struggles more than I wish: fear, doubt, and negativity. The writer told of an evangelistic meeting in Ireland where the speaker was explaining about abiding in Christ and trusting him completely and unconditionally, no matter the circumstance. My reading speed slowed immediately so that I could drink deeply of the words I needed as much as a thirsty, exhausted traveler craves water in the desert. I was especially drawn to the speaker's concluding thought in his message about how abiding and trusting in Jesus "means that in every circumstance you can keep on saying, 'For this I have Jesus.'"

Some people think seeking Jesus in difficult times means that they themselves are weak. (And who likes to be weak and vulnerable?) But Jesus tried to correct such a mistaken idea by saying, "It is not the healthy who need a doctor, but the sick" (Matthew 9:12). In other words, when we recognize and admit our sickness—physical, emotional, and/or spiritual—we are blessed because we know where we can find help. Reassured and comforted, our hearts resound, "For this I have Jesus."

In my case, all signs are that I'm not doing too well physically. I'm lacking in energy and "get up and go" (as my mother would say), losing weight, unable to sleep well, and suffering from pain and weakness, especially in my legs. Generally I'm feeling quite distant from the me I used to know and be. (Who is that person in the mirror whose hair is turning gray faster than a proud kindergartener can count from one to ten?) It's hard to keep my thoughts from running ahead of what I know (that God is fully and completely in control) and what I only conjecture whenever I feel a small twinge of pain (that cancer is taking over my body).

But in all of this I remember, "For this I have Jesus." And I rejoice in God's faithfulness in the midst of this now twenty-month-old cancer journey. How could I walk it alone? I'm so grateful I don't have to.

"Because of the LORD's great love we are not consumed, for his compassions never fail. They are new every morning; great is your faithfulness. I say to myself, 'The LORD is my portion; therefore I will wait for him" (Lamentations 3:22–24).

To Ponder: For this _____ (fill in the blank) I have Jesus.

To Pray: Loving heavenly Father, I offer my joyful praise to you because of who you are. Continue to reveal yourself to me, I pray, so that I may know you more intimately, worship you more sincerely, and bring you honor and glory without ceasing until sunset. In Jesus' name, amen.

AFTERTHOUGHT

In looking back over this incredible cancer journey, I'm grateful for so much, especially the lessons God is teaching me daily. Some of these are lessons yet in progress. For a good dose of encouragement, here are ten significant lessons:*

Patience. I'd far rather just jump right to healing, but it's been nearly two years of wait, wait, and wait some more. I'm still waiting. After the cancer recurred, I had to wait a very long three-plus weeks before starting the first anticancer medicine. Every two weeks thereafter, I waited for test results to show if the drug was being effective. When in March 2010 a CT scan showed that the drug had stopped working, I had to wait another seemingly endless three weeks to start the second drug. What really tested my patience (and faith) was that throughout this wait my body was weakening noticeably. There is a lot of stop and start on this journey. I'd rather just keep going forward, but...

God is worthy of praise. Always. Forever. No matter what CT scans and blood tests show and doctors proclaim. No matter how I feel. No matter what. None of these change or challenge the always faithful, always powerful, always in control God.

---

* These Bible passages are some that support the lessons God has been teaching me during this journey: Psalm 27:14; Habakkuk 3:17–18; Hebrews 13:8; Psalm 46:1– 2, 10; Isaiah 40:30–31; Philippians 4:8; 1 John 3:1; Psalm 37:4–7.

My trust is in God. It is not in percentages, the efficacy rate of a certain drug, the chances that surgery, if even possible, will get all of the cancer, survival rates for renal cell carcinoma, and more. My trust is in God, my Father, whose Word never fails.

Doctors don't know everything. Even their guesses—educated though they may be—are only guesses. Will this particular medicine work? What treatment is best? Should they perform surgery? How about radiation? How long will I live? Only God knows. I am so happy that my trust is in him.

My husband stands beside me "for better, for worse, in sickness, in health." Never have my wedding vows been so meaningful; never has Bernie's love been so real. I don't have cancer—we have cancer. We travel the journey and fight the battle together.

The family of God is truly amazing. How frequently Bernie has commented that the prayers of the family of God around the world provide the updraft for the eagle to soar. A prayer partner in Missouri said it a different way when she wrote, "When you can't pray, remember that we're praying for you."

The cancer journey shouldn't be walked alone. It's a journey for the whole family—both one's blood family and the wider family of God. Why would anyone choose to bear the burden silently while trying to keep a stiff upper lip and a smile on the face? Why would anyone choose to walk alone? It happens often in Japan, where people are so private about personal matters, but the cancer walk should not be attempted alone.

God's Word is powerful and full of promise and hope. Scripture is the way God has spoken to me most often along the way. I've been renewed, strengthened, comforted, challenged, nourished, and sometimes chastised. Matthew 4:4 reminds us we don't live by bread alone. Neither do I live by anticancer medicines. Far more important is the Word of God—something I've "known" my whole life, but never as I've known it recently.

Don't forget what is truly important. Although cancer is a deadly disease, it isn't the most important thing in my life. So I've chosen not to focus on the cancer itself. (I leave this to the doctors.) Instead, I want to focus on the Lord and on walking with him. Philippians 4:8 is good advice—the very best.

My worth doesn't stem from what I do. It is based on who I am: God's beloved child. So many scriptures testify to this fact, yet I confess I've often acted as if the more productive I am, the more worthy I am. According to my date book, I've not accomplished much so far in the journey. Instead, I've been with the Lord in his school of learning. I have a much clearer understanding of God. I stand on a foundation that cannot be moved. It's a new kind of productivity that I've discovered: delighting myself at Jesus' feet even if I accomplish nothing else during the day. It is enough.

CPSIA information can be obtained at www.ICGtesting.com
Printed in the USA
LVOW05s2026010813

345755LV00001B/2/P